The POWER OF AFFIRMATIONS *and* POSITIVE SELF-TALK

BOB BAKER

SPOTLIGHT PUBLICATIONS

BobBakerInspiration.com

The Power of Affirmations and Positive Self-Talk
Bob Baker

ISBN: 978-1-7367053-0-8
© 2021 Bob Baker — All Rights Reserved
Published by Spotlight Publications and BobBakerInspiration.com
PO Box 28441, St. Louis, MO 63146, USA

Disclaimer: This book is designed to provide information and inspiration to help people develop a more positive attitude and outlook on life. It is sold with the understanding that the publisher and author are not engaged in rendering therapeutic, psychological, or other professional services. If other expert assistance is required, the services of a competent professional should be sought.

It is not the purpose of this book to cover the full range of information that is otherwise available on this topic, but instead to complement, amplify, and supplement other texts. You are urged to read all available material and tailor the information to your individual needs.

Every effort has been made to make this book as accurate as possible. However, there may be mistakes, and some details may be inaccurate by the time you read this. Therefore, this text should be used only as a general guide and not as the ultimate source of information on the topic.

The author and publisher shall have neither liability nor responsibility to any person or entity with respect to any loss or damage caused, or alleged to have been caused, directly or indirectly, by the information contained in this book.

Photo credits: Cover image © Netfalls stock.adobe.com; p. 8-9 © Obeyleesin stock. adobe.com; p. 10 Forest Storyblocks.com; p. 21 Mountains Storyblocks.com; p. 29 © Subbotina Dreamstime.com; p. 37 © Frenta Dreamstime.com; p. 45 Bumble bee Storyblocks.com; p. 54-55 © Netfalls stock.adobe.com; p. 56 © hiro.y stock.adobe. com; p. 59 Oat field Storyblocks.com; p. 63 Sunflowers Storyblocks.com; p. 68 Ferns Storyblocks.com; p. 73 Fresh herbs Storyblocks.com; p. 78 © Maridave stock.adobe. com; p. 82 Golden meadow Storyblocks.com; p. 85 © Rabbit75_fot stock.adobe.com.

Editorial Support by Andrew Doty for Editwright, *Editwright.com*
Design by Monica Thomas for TLC Book Design, *TLCBookDesign.com*

Printed in the United States of America

*JEN,
IT'S BEEN SO FUN GETTING
TO KNOW YOU, THANKS FOR
BEING A BRIGHT LIGHT IN
THE WORLD!*

*APRIL
2021*

*To my many YouTube subscribers—
Your interest and attention launched a whole
new chapter of my life. I am forever grateful
for your kind words and encouragement.
This book and my continuing mission to
inspire people like you to live your best life
are fueled by your support.*

Thank you!

Also by Bob Baker

The Empowered Artist

The Passion Principles

Guerrilla Music Marketing Handbook

The Improv Comedy Musician
(with Laura Hall)

*Personal and Spiritual Growth
for Fun People*

Unleash the Artist Within

The DIY Career Manifesto

Branding Yourself Online

The Five-Minute Music Marketer

The 9 Irrefutable Laws of Music Marketing

The Guerrilla Guide to Book Marketing

LET'S CONNECT!

If you enjoy this book and want to apply the power of affirmations to your life even more, here are a few ways to do that:

- Subscribe to my YouTube channel at www. YouTube.com/BobBaker, where I publish two new affirmation and meditation videos every week.

- Get six free affirmation MP3 downloads when you visit my website at www.BobBakerInspiration.com.

- Stream my affirmations on Spotify, Apple Music, and most audio platforms. Just search for my artist name, Bob Baker's Inspiration Project.

- Check out the *Affirmation Meditation Podcast with Bob Baker*, available on Apple Podcasts, Spotify, Amazon Music, Audible, and most podcasting apps.

CONTENTS

Section 1

THE FOUNDATION

This is the heart of the book, where I share my personal growth journey and how I discovered the power of directing my thoughts to create the life I wanted. You'll learn how affirmations work and why they are so powerful.

I also share tips and best practices on how to create your own affirmative statements, when and where to use them, how often, and more.

Buckle up and get ready to turbocharge your life!

Chapter 1

LET'S GET STARTED

Welcome to a little book that could very well change your life!

I don't make that boastful claim lightly. Having experienced the power of positive self-talk firsthand in my own life, and after having witnessed its impact on the lives of countless people around the world, I can state that with confidence.

My YouTube channel, which features hundreds of affirmation videos, attracts half a million unique viewers every month. These good people, from all over the globe, have left tens of thousands of comments. The vast majority proclaim how much their lives have improved as a result of being intentional about the internal messages they tell themselves.

Indeed, the conversations you have in your own head have a tremendous impact on your attitude and outlook. And that enhanced state of mind leads to inspired actions and tangible results.

So, whether you are exploring the idea of affirmations for the first time or you are wanting to reinforce an existing belief in their effectiveness, this is the resource for you.

A quick note if you are completely new to affirmations

What are they? Affirmations are positive statements you say to yourself, either out loud or in your mind. They can address a variety of topics and aspects of your life. Some examples include:

"I am grateful for the many blessings in my life."

"Today I look for the good — in myself and other people."

"I am worthy. I am enough."

You can create your own affirmations and write them down. Some people also seek out affirmation recordings, like the ones I publish on YouTube. With these, you can recite the affirmations back to yourself or simply listen and imagine how each statement will impact your life.

The autopilot conundrum and my personal story

Most people live their lives as if their minds and circumstances are on autopilot. Good and bad things randomly happen to them. Emotions unexpectedly creep up, out of their control. Reactions to people and events automatically occur, because that's their "reality."

It's not a crime to live that way. People simply don't know any better. We're not taught these things in school and we often don't get the proper insights from our parents. There is no "how to use your mind" instruction manual given to us when we reach a certain age or maturity.

That was definitely the case when I was a child. I was raised by a single mother in a lower-middle-class neighborhood. My mom was incredibly supportive and loving, but she was a quiet, shy person. She never owned a car and worked for many years at a nonprofit with a modest salary. Money was always tight.

Like many kids that age, I lacked confidence and self-worth in grade school and well into high school. I had a few friends I was comfortable with, but much of the time I felt socially awkward. And since I was not particularly good at sports, I got picked on and made fun of in physical education classes, which spilled over into other areas of school life.

These circumstances forced me to become self-reliant and find joy on my own. I was my mom's only child, so I found ways to occupy my time alone. That led to getting involved in music, writing, art, and more — interests that shape my life to this day.

Even though I was cultivating these creative interests, I still felt insecure. My nervousness in social situations often brought out a stutter in my speech, which made me even more self-conscious and timid.

When I got into high school, I started playing the guitar, singing, and even playing music publicly.

That led to more social acceptance from my peers and instilled some confidence in my new identity as a musician. But I still battled with thoughts and feelings of inadequacy.

Like so many people, I believed those thoughts and feelings were simply who I was. They were coming from my mind. I felt them in my body. They must be real.

And that's exactly how most people live their lives on autopilot — letting their thoughts and emotions run wild, then hanging on for dear life as they try to cope. Can you relate?

The turning point

Then something unexpected happened in my junior year of high school. I was spending time with my friend Gary Miller during one particularly rough patch. I was wrestling with inner turmoil and frustration, and he knew it.

"Here's a book I read that was very helpful," Gary said. "You are welcome to borrow it. It might help you too."

That book was *Your Erroneous Zones* by Wayne Dyer. And, I have to say, reading it changed my life.

There's a good chance you've heard of Wayne Dyer. *Your Erroneous Zones* came out in 1976 and was his first bestseller. He went on to publish dozens of titles, many with a spiritual theme. But his first few books fell more into the positive thinking and pop psychology category. Sadly, in 2015, he passed away at age 75.

What blew my mind was Dyer's assertion that our thoughts and feelings are not an accurate reflection of who we truly are. That book made me aware, for the first time, that I can take control of the conversations going on in my own head.

I didn't have to passively accept all aspects of my inner dialogue. I could choose to keep the thoughts that served me (such as "I am a good guitar player and singer.") and discard and replace the thoughts that did not serve me (such as "She doesn't want to talk to me. I'm a loser.").

That blew my mind!

I was also astonished to learn about this sequence of events: I can monitor my inner dialogue and notice when my thoughts are positive versus negative. I can then choose to think thoughts that empower me. Those positive thoughts then influence my feelings and emotions, which then steer my actions and behavior, which directly impact the results and circumstances of my life.

Wow!

After coming to this realization, I was no longer a victim held hostage by whatever negative idea happened to pop into my head. I was in the driver's seat of my mind — and my life!

Don't get me wrong. I didn't instantly become Superman and live happily ever after. I had years of low self-esteem patterns to work through. But coming to these realizations began a lifelong journey of self-discovery and personal growth that continues to this day.

Along the way, I learned about and implemented several important behaviors, such as:

- Being clear about what I want
- Writing down my goals
- Reading and listening to inspiring material
- Surrounding myself with positive people
- Taking action on my inspired ideas

I also experimented with these powerful techniques:

- Visualization
- Meditation
- Mindfulness

But it was affirmations and positive self-talk that became the foundation of my development and personal growth.

Like most people, I haven't employed these habits every day for years on end. My daily routines ebb and flow with life. But I've focused on them consistently enough to have greatly influenced my accomplishments and the course of my life.

The results

Taking control of my conscious thoughts lead to some pretty amazing things. In my mid-twenties I started a music magazine and ended up publishing it for 10 years. In my early thirties, my first book was published. I have since written and published 15 paperbacks and dozens more titles in e-book, audiobook, and online course formats.

One of my books, *Guerrilla Music Marketing Handbook*, appeared in the movie *School of Rock*, starring Jack Black. Berklee College of Music in Boston approached me to create an online course called "Music Marketing 101." I've appeared in the press on NPR, *The Guardian*, *Publishers Weekly*, and many more media outlets around the world.

Along the way I overcame my social awkwardness and ended up doing stand-up comedy, acting in dozens of plays, and performing with improv comedy groups.

I've been blessed to live a rich, active life. And I truly believe knowing how to use my mind properly allowed me to enjoy all of these experiences.

The YouTube era

That's why, in 2016, it was not out of character for me to record some spoken-word affirmations and upload them to my YouTube channel. I had been using affirmations for many years and knew the potential power they held.

I had no grand plan for these new recordings, but I was curious if they would appeal to anyone. I had been podcasting since 2005 and, being a singer and performer, I was comfortable speaking into a microphone. I knew how to record, edit, and upload audio and video files. So, with a sense of play and experimentation, I decided to put some of this material out there.

However, I admit I was also nervous because this new type of content was quite different from my usual tips for musicians and creative types. I braced myself for some backlash.

But no backlash ever came. And the new affirmation videos started getting more views than my typical content. Nothing went viral right off the bat, but it was a clear signal that there was an interest in this type of material. Also, many people seemed to enjoy the tone of my voice.

In short order, I felt a growing calling to create more of these inspirational recordings. I remember the thrill of seeing my YouTube channel grow to 20,000 subscribers. Within six months, that number doubled. Six months later, it doubled again.

In late 2019, I hit 100,000 subscribers. In the summer of 2020 I surpassed one million views per month across the entire channel. Consistently posting two new inspirational videos a week for the last few years has opened up a whole new chapter of my life and career, far surpassing anything I experienced as an accomplished author.

The numbers are nice to celebrate, and they continue to boggle my mind. But what really lights me up is knowing I am helping to improve the lives of hundreds of thousands of people around the world. It's a testimony to the power of affirmations and positive self-talk!

That's why I'm so excited to share this message with you.

Chapter 2

WHY AFFIRMATIONS ARE SO POWERFUL

The influence of positive self-talk can be summed up in this short quote I've always attributed to Wayne Dyer (although I don't recall where I first saw it):

"What you focus on expands in your life."

It's a simple idea, yet incredibly powerful. What you put your attention on will often manifest in your reality.

Even though I first discovered the concept of taking control of my thoughts through one of Dyer's early books, he was not the first person to promote this idea. Far from it.

In 1956, Earl Nightingale published a vinyl audio recording called *The Strangest Secret*, which sold a million copies and launched a new spoken-word audio industry.

Nightingale's main message in that classic recording, and a phrase he repeated many times throughout his life, was this:

"We become what we think about most of the time."

And, if you want to go way back in time, there's this verse from the Book of Proverbs in the Bible:

"As he thinketh in his heart, so is he."

Author James Allen liked that verse so much, he used part of it as the title of a book he published in 1903.

Here's how Allen described his book, *As a Man Thinketh*:

"It shows how, in his own thought-world,
each man holds the key to every condition,
good or bad, that enters into his life, and that,

by working patiently and intelligently upon
his thoughts, he may remake his life, and
transform his circumstances."

If you overlook the outdated use of the male pronoun
and the stiff writing style, you'll discover the powerful principle behind this topic:

*Your dominant thoughts are the driving force behind
your attitude, actions, and results!*

How and why affirmations work

Several years ago I bought a Honda Element. It's
a box-shaped vehicle with a unique look. Prior to
purchasing the car, I had not given much thought to
that make and model. But after owning the car and
loving it, I started seeing Honda Elements every-
where I went.

It was uncanny. Where were all these vehicles sud-
denly coming from? Did I unknowingly start a new
trend? Of course not.

Honda Elements were there the whole time. They
were all around me before and after I purchased one.

It's just that I never noticed them until that distinct make and model was top of mind within me.

Here's the thing ...

Every day our brains are bombarded with sensory stimulation. Sights, sounds, smells, tastes, physical sensations, and thousands of random thoughts.

Your human brain can't possibly process all of that information. It isn't equipped to do that. So your mind was designed to filter out most of it so it can focus on what is most important.

How does your mind decide what to focus on?

Whether you are aware of it or not, your brain develops a filter. This filter is the shield that determines what information to discard and what to let in.

Your brain uses many factors to create this mental filter, including:

- Your past experiences
- Your family and upbringing
- Your religious and spiritual beliefs

- Your friends and coworkers
- The music, books, movies, video games, and entertainment you expose yourself to
- Your predominant thoughts
- And much more

Your mental algorithm

Here's another way to think of it in a modern context. Let's use YouTube in this example, since there's a good chance that's how you discovered my affirmation work. But this principle also applies to Facebook, Amazon, and most social media platforms.

When you watch videos on YouTube, the site tracks your behavior. It monitors what videos you watch, what topics you enjoy, and how much time you spend watching. For better or worse, the technology running silently in the background is trying to determine what you are interested in.

YouTube and other sites do this because they want to deliver the best personalized experience for you. The more satisfied you are while on the site, the more time you'll spend there, and the more customized content and ads they can serve you.

Therefore, if you watch a lot of videos on yoga poses, training a Yorkshire Terrier, and healthy vegan recipes, every time you open up YouTube, you'll see a lot of suggestions for more videos on those topics.

Why is this helpful? Because you can't possibly sift through all of the millions of videos on YouTube, just like your brain can't comprehend all the sensory information around you. So, YouTube creates filters to help you.

Again, what YouTube is doing is serving more of the content you want, based on your previous behavior. If you stop watching yoga videos and start watching weight lifting videos instead, within a short time, YouTube will stop suggesting yoga and start showing you more content related to weight lifting.

You might see where I'm going with this. In essence, your mind works in an amazingly similar way. Based on your habits and predominant thought patterns, your brain develops a filter that serves up more of what you focus on.

Like YouTube, it uses your most recent thoughts, emotions, and activities to develop and solidify this filter.

For instance, if you think the government is out to get you, your filter will show you plenty of examples to reinforce that belief. If you feel that most people are basically good, you'll see an abundance of examples all around you to support that belief.

The more examples you see on a given topic, and the more often you percolate with thoughts and feelings related to that perspective, the more potent your beliefs about that thing become. Just like building a muscle, you make that aspect of your filter stronger.

This explains why I started seeing Honda Elements after I purchased one. It also explains how two people can look at the same event and come to different conclusions. Their filters influence their perception of "reality."

As I mentioned before, most human beings are not even aware that there is a filter through which they view the world. They firmly believe "It is what it is."

But not you, because you are now keenly aware that you have a filter and that it is greatly impacting your life.

If you're happy with your filter and your life, then carry on and enjoy yourself.

But if you think you could be living a happier, more fulfilling life, then put some time and energy into altering your mental filter.

You can intentionally upgrade your filter

Earlier I mentioned how YouTube changes what it shows you based on your most recent viewing habits. By changing your viewing behavior and what videos you seek out, over time the algorithm will adjust and serve up different suggestions.

In the same way, you can influence how your filter behaves and what information gets in through it. In other words, you can transform your filter to become a tool that empowers you instead of hinders you!

The main thing I want you to realize is that you are not stuck with your current attitude, outlook, and circumstances. You can make a decision, right now, to take control of your thoughts, upgrade your filter, and change your life for the better.

And affirmations are a powerful tool to help you accomplish that!

Chapter 3

WHAT ABOUT THE LAW OF ATTRACTION?

There's a good chance you've come across the phrase "Law of Attraction" at some point. The term was first used in the 1800s by a variety of authors who fall into a philosophical category known as New Thought. It was a fresh perspective on the power of the individual to use their mind to positively influence their health, wealth, happiness, and more.

The idea continued to be discussed throughout the 1900s as self-help books and recordings became more popular. The Law of Attraction achieved great prominence in the mid-2000s with the success of the movie and book, *The Secret*.

There are different views on this law, many of which focus on the role of energy and vibration. The underlying premise: If you feed your mind with positive thoughts and mental images, you raise your personal vibration and frequency.

Many people believe when you emit a positive vibration, it radiates out into the world and attracts to you the people and circumstances you want. The right person sits next to you on the subway, the perfect book is on display in the window of a bookstore you happen to walk by, etc.

What I believe

Years ago I adopted a perspective that has served me well throughout my life: I readily admit I don't know all the answers.

I do not now (and may not ever) know exactly how everything works. And I am totally comfortable with that. I do have strong values and opinions on many topics, but I also have an open mind when it comes to the great mysteries of life.

Many people feel tortured when they don't know all the answers about God, life, spirit, and the soul. To relieve the pressure, they adopt specific belief systems that provide answers. There's nothing wrong with that, but some people take it to an extreme and become so rigid in knowing the answers that they dismiss other views and people who have come to different conclusions.

Personally, I love science and value evidence-based findings from reputable experts and media sources. I also enjoy exploring a variety of spiritual outlooks and practices. I have many friends who are practitioners in yoga, massage, Reiki, and other energy and healing arts.

I'm open-minded about all of them, while also not clinging too tightly to any one belief. As long as someone's belief doesn't harm other people or property, I'm very accepting and wish them well.

How does this relate to the Law of Attraction?

To answer that question, let's imagine for a moment that you are single and desire to have a romantic partner in your life. Every day, for weeks on end, you visualize yourself with an ideal person and repeat affirmations such as, "I deserve a loving, respectful partner."

One night you go to your weekly book club meeting and a new man or woman attends. You end up sitting next to each other and strike up a conversation. You get along great and weeks later go on your first date.

So, what happened with this scenario?

Did you send a vibrational signal out into the world that caused this person to attend the meeting? Did a magnetic force compel them to sit next to you?

Perhaps it did. And I think it would be wonderful if the Universe works that way. I'm very open to the possibility that it does.

But what if it doesn't work that way? What if affirmations and positive self-talk work on a purely practical and personal level?

Maybe your daily affirmation practice caused your mental filter to be on the lookout for a potential partner, so you immediately noticed this new person when they entered the room.

And, since you were feeling more positive about yourself (because you'd been reciting daily affirmations), you were relaxed and had a friendly look on your face. That influenced the person to feel comfortable enough to sit next to you.

In this scenario, your future dating partner wasn't compelled to attend by some unseen force. They would have attended no matter what. But, because you had been doing the work to improve your mindset, you were much more open and receptive to noticing them and engaging with them in a positive manner.

Does this second, more practical scenario diminish the process?

To me, it's every bit as powerful and amazing!

So, no matter what your thoughts are on affirmations and why they work, I sincerely hope you embrace them.

If you are leery about the Law of Attraction aspect, please don't discount the effectiveness of positive self-talk. It works on a very grounded level. When you positively firm up your personal filter, it directly influences how you show up in the world. You are then open to seeing more opportunities and inter-acting with other people in a more empowering way.

If, on the other hand, you believe your positive thoughts send out vibrational waves that influence the physical world, I applaud you as well. As long as that belief serves you, keep using it!

And, if you're like me, and you're not completely sure how it all works, relax. Just know that feeding your mind with uplifting messages regularly will benefit you and improve your life — whether you know how it works or not!

Choose your delusion

Here's a warning: Don't be surprised if you encoun-ter cynical people who believe doing affirmations is some airy-fairy thing that only New Age hippies do.

These opinionated people will say you are "burying your head in the sand" or viewing life "through rose-colored glasses."

They may tell you the world is a depressing place, that you should accept this negative "reality," and that trying to be a shiny, happy person is delusional.

Heck, there's a good chance you have had these same thoughts yourself.

This may surprise you, but to a degree, I agree with that outlook. Life at times is filled with challenges and tragedy, and to be responsible humans we should acknowledge those less-than-pleasant aspects.

And I agree that happy people are "delusional." But I also believe negative people are just as delusional. In many ways, every human being is delusional.

What do I mean by that?

We all have our own individual perceptions of "reality." Things exist and things happen, but it's up to each person to give them meaning.

Yes, most rational people agree on many topics, such as not condoning or engaging in harming others. That should go without saying. But when it comes to the more mundane events of our lives — which make up the bulk of our human experience — there is a wide diversity of perspectives.

I think I've made it abundantly clear by now: We all view the world through a lens of our own making. That's why one person will view getting fired from a job as a burden, while someone else will view it as an opportunity. Neither person is "right." Both are being delusional, based on their unique point of view.

I even happily believe my own perspective is delusional. Why does that thrill me? Because if we're all creating a personalized story in our minds ...

Why not choose a delusion that will help you be more happy and joyful?

Why live your brief appearance on earth in turmoil or with apathy, when you can choose to live it with energy and enthusiasm?

If you're going to be delusional anyway, choose a delusion that serves you, serves others, and leaves the world a better place.

This isn't a point of view you will hear a lot of the self-help gurus express. But it's a perspective that works for me. I hope you find it helpful too.

Chapter 4

DEVELOPING A DAILY AFFIRMATION ROUTINE

One thing I've come to realize after running a popular YouTube channel filled with hundreds of affirmation videos is that most people seek out these types of recordings when they are hurting. They might be going through a financial or health challenge, a relationship breakup, or other low point in life.

If that's how you discovered me or this book, congratulations. You took an important step toward improving your life, and you should feel good about that. Hopefully, incorporating affirmations into your life has made (or will soon make) a positive impact on you.

Just note that, once you start feeling better, you may drift away from using affirmations and feeding your mind with positive messages. There's nothing wrong with that. I've gotten away from it at times in my own life.

But one thing I've noticed over the years is that when I engage in a daily practice of affirmations (combined with meditation, journaling, visualization, and goal setting), my life is better. I feel more focused and energized. As a result, I get things done and make more progress.

That's why I highly recommend you develop a daily affirmation practice — in good times and bad. It will keep you sharp and upbeat, and it will have a power-ful effect on the mental filter that influences your life.

Make it easy

Maintaining this practice doesn't have to be burden-some or time-consuming. The great news is that an affirmation routine can be very flexible and adaptable.

Short on time? You can still benefit from spending just five minutes counting your blessings or visualizing your ideal day. Certainly, you can find five minutes to devote to your well-being. Right?

Also, how and where you recite affirmations is up to you. If you have a meditation room or space, and you like to sit with your eyes closed, do it. But you can also listen and say them while you walk, drive, work out, or clean the house.

Also, you don't have to listen to the same recording every day, unless you want to. Mix them up. I have hundreds to choose from on my YouTube channel, and you can find many more from other people.

Create a YouTube or Spotify playlist of your favorites. Listen to one at a time or three in a row. I hope you're getting the point: There are no strict rules. Find a system that works for you. And anytime you want to change things up, go for it.

The most important thing

The only aspect of your new affirmation practice that I ask you to do in a specific way is the "routine" part. You can approach it any way you want, as long as you develop and maintain a daily habit. Yes, affirmations should ideally be done DAILY — at least once, and more often if you can swing it.

If you get off track and miss a day or two, don't beat yourself up. Just jump back in and commit to the regular practice. Doing so will have a profound influence on your mindset and quality of life.

I want to stress this one more time: Continue your daily affirmation practice when life is good, bad, and ugly. As I said before, people tend to engage in positive self-talk to get through a tough time. Once things get better and the pressure is off, there's a tendency to stray from the routine.

But please resist that tendency and commit to your ongoing empowerment! It will help you weather the ups and downs that inevitably happen in life.

Let's compare the process to getting in good physical shape. Imagine you go to the gym three times a week for six months. You transform your body and feel great. You have arrived at an optimal state of health.

What would happen if you stopped exercising? You know the answer. You would maintain your heightened physical appearance for a while, but before long your body would return to its previous state.

The same principle applies to strengthening your mindset and your filter. It needs and deserves constant care and feeding. All the more reason to commit to a daily practice and make it part of your lifestyle.

Moving past awkwardness and doubt

A quick note if you are new to doing affirmations: The first few times you recite positive statements to yourself, it may seem odd. You might feel silly and think to yourself, "This is ridiculous. How can this possibly help me?" I admit I had the same thoughts many years ago when I first did them.

But stick with it. You will move past that awkward feeling, and the benefit waiting for you on the other side is well worth it.

If you've ever taken piano or guitar lessons, you know this concept well. At first, everything is uncomfortable and mechanical. But little by little, as you get the hang of it, things become more fluid as you begin to enjoy your newfound abilities.

Also, the affirmations you recite must feel authentic. They must ring true for you.

If you are literally down to your last dollar, and you state, "I am a millionaire," your brain will scream, "No, you're not!" Having that mismatch in your mind could end up making you feel worse instead of better.

I do believe that a "fake it till you make it" approach can work, whereby you emphatically state affirmations based on where you are heading — not where you are. But I also think for some people it's best to choose affirmations that feel more authentic in the moment.

For example, stating, "I am happy" or "I love my life" might not feel right if you've been going through a bout of depression.

Consider these affirmations instead:

"I am open to allowing more joy into my life."

"I am ready for a new relationship with my emotions."

Don't those ring true? Even if you are feeling down, aren't you open to the possibility of experiencing more joy? Aren't you genuinely ready to feel a new set of emotions?

So, choose affirmations (whether on a recording or written yourself) that reflect where you are combined with where you want to be.

The best times to do affirmations

You already know that establishing a daily practice will produce the greatest long-term benefit. But what time of the day should you ideally devote to doing affirmations?

The short answer is: at any time of the day you will consistently incorporate it into your life. Again, developing an affirmation habit is your ultimate goal.

However, beyond that, I believe the best time to recite affirmations is first thing in the morning. That's when your mind is most relaxed and you haven't jumped into the details of your responsibilities and to-do list.

Also, doing them that early sets the foundation for the rest of your day. It's time you devote to yourself every morning (or whichever part of the day you arise) to set an intention. Instead of launching into your day and immediately reacting to circumstances, you take a breath and focus on the outcomes you want to create.

So, if you can carve out just one time slot per day for affirmations, morning would be my first choice.

If you can squeeze in a second session, right before bedtime would be ideal. That way, you affirm the mindset you desire as you drift off to sleep and once more right after you awake. It's the perfect bookend structure for your daily affirmation practice.

If you really want to turbocharge things, find times to recite positive statements during the day too. Especially if you are just starting a practice or going through a tough time, pour it on. As long as you feel you benefit from the repetition, do affirmations as frequently as you want.

Chapter 5

AFFIRMATION BEST PRACTICES AND MISTAKES TO AVOID

Having worked with affirmations for decades, and being a writer who loves language, I know there are many ways to phrase affirmations. And, while I don't want to burden you with too many affirmation "rules," there are some pitfalls I recommend you steer clear of.

The purpose of affirmations is to get your conscious and subconscious mind to focus on what you want, instead of what you don't want. For instance, consider this statement:

"Today I will not let the negative people in my life get me down."

I understand the intention behind a sentence like that, but look at the key words: "will not," "negative people," "get me down." Reciting an affirmation like that will only reinforce the frustration you feel from not having more supportive people in your life.

The good news is, a statement like that can be easily reworded to serve you better:

"Today I will stay grounded and look for the good in the people I encounter."

That's a much more powerful statement. It is laser-focused on the outcome you really want. The earlier version might help you survive and get through your day, but the latter version compels you to thrive instead.

This is a more subtle piece of advice, but try to avoid statements like "I want more money" or "I can't wait to finally earn more income." These types of statements unintentionally emphasize the wanting and how the money is just out of reach.

Instead, say something like, "I recognize the abundance that flows all around me" or "Abundance is my birthright and I claim it now."

Bottom line: If you write your own affirmations, pay close attention to how they are worded and make sure they focus on the positive outcomes you desire.

Keep the focus on you

Another mistake I've seen many times is when people set an intention about someone else's behavior.

Examples:

"Jimmy is now getting good grades in school."

"Emily is attracted to me and wants to go on a date."

Those may be things you desire, but you have no control over how Jimmy and Emily feel or what they do. Affirmations like that will disappoint you more often than not.

Your affirmation statements should be about you and things you have control over. Therefore, create affirmations that reinforce a quality you can personally embody that might lead to similar outcomes.

Examples:

"I recognize Jimmy's intelligence, offer encouragement, and do my best to provide an environment where he can thrive."

"I am a kind and loving person who is worthy of having a mate who loves and appreciates me."

These statements focus on what you do and how you feel, which are things you can directly influence. Make sure all of your affirmations serve the same purpose.

Speaking, thinking, hearing, reading, writing

There are many ways to experience affirmations. Speak them out loud, say them in your mind, listen to them, read them, or write them down. You can also combine one or more of these methods.

For instance, with my affirmation audio recordings, you will hear me state each affirmation. Then, I usually leave space for you to repeat it back to yourself. This approach impacts you on two levels: entering through your ears, then being reinforced by your own voice.

I realize that sometimes, if other people are nearby, you have no choice but to recite affirmations in your head. And that's fine. But if you have the option, saying them out loud can be more powerful. Whenever you can, state them with your voice — loud and proud. Engaging your vocal cords and your body will allow the statements to penetrate even deeper.

You can also add another physical dimension by writing out your favorite affirmations by hand. For instance, after you listen to an affirmation recording, grab a journal and write down the statements that stood out for you. This will further reinforce the meaning behind the affirmations.

Here's another great way to remind yourself of the positive thoughts you want to focus on: Print out your favorite affirmations and pin them up where you will see them throughout your day. Place them on the bathroom mirror, on the refrigerator, in your car, on your computer, etc.

You get the idea: Bombard your mind, body, and soul with the positive thoughts and empowering attitudes you want to embody.

Two secret ingredients

Finally, let's talk about two factors that will have the greatest impact on the real-world results you enjoy because of your affirmation practice.

First, do your best to feel as much emotion and enthusiasm as you can when you recite your positive statements.

Think about your most vivid memories and the events of your life that shaped you. It's safe to say those moments were filled with strong emotions.

It may have been the birth of a child or the loss of someone close to you. Perhaps it was winning an award, getting married, facing a serious health threat, or experiencing a major breakthrough.

When you feel intense feelings of loss, sadness, or anger — as well as feelings of joy, accomplishment, or love — those experiences get solidified within you and greatly influence your beliefs moving forward.

Whether you are aware of it or not, your emotions color that mental filter we've talked so much about in this book. That explains why you may feel confident in business but insecure with romance — or vice versa. Or passionate about art and frustrated by traditional day jobs — or vice versa.

I know it's not always easy to manufacture emotion, but when you recite your affirmations, really lean into them. Say them with gusto. Do your best to summon the feeling you want to experience related to the statement you are expressing.

You can also attach each affirmation to a memory. If you enthusiastically exclaim, "I am happy," think of a time in your life when you deeply felt happy. Tap into your existing internal library of experiences.

And the second crucial ingredient to making the most of an affirmation practice:

The new beliefs you install in your mind must lead to inspired action!

Your intentions will come to life when your positive thoughts transmute into new behaviors in the physical, 3D world.

If that idea feels overwhelming, here's some good news: The actions you take don't have to be monumental. A simple shift in your daily habits over time can have a profound effect on your circumstances.

Whether you want to improve your health, find a partner, create a new income source, or be more compassionate, you can make progress toward your goals incrementally.

That's exactly how I grew my YouTube channel. I committed to publishing two new videos every week. I did that consistently for months on end. That dedication to taking action paid off. It led to me writing this book and to you reading it.

And what about the hundreds of books, podcasts, blog posts, and courses I've created over the years? They didn't write themselves. I had to sit down and focus on one idea, one sentence, and one section at a time.

You can do the same thing. Baby steps, taken consistently over time, lead to dramatic positive results in your life.

So, commit to a daily affirmation practice. Engage your senses by speaking the statements, hearing them, reading them, writing them down, and feeling them with emotion.

Bombard your mind with positive messages, and use your newfound enthusiasm to take action and interact with other people in the real world.

That's when you'll become a manifestation master!

Section 2

THE AFFIRMATIONS

Now that you've laid the foundation for your affirmation practice, this section offers a series of powerful affirmations in seven categories: gratitude, positivity, joy, confidence, health, love, and abundance.

There are many ways to use these affirmations: read them, recite them out loud, write them down, print them, place them where you will see them throughout your day. The idea is to immerse yourself in the thoughts and feelings that will allow you to live a purposeful life.

You can also listen to the affirmations in this section using the audio version of this book. And for variety, you'll find many more recordings (hundreds of them) on my YouTube channel at www.YouTube.com/BobBaker. Click the Playlist tab to find videos separated by topic.

Affirmations 1

START YOUR DAY WITH GRATITUDE

There's no doubt about it. Being thankful for what you have is the best way to allow more abundance, love, joy, and fulfillment into your life.

Take a moment right now to get centered. Take a couple of slow, deep breaths in and out. Just clear your mind as you prepare to repeat these powerful affirmations back to yourself.

Let's begin.

I am grateful to be alive.

I am grateful for where I am right now.

I am grateful for all I have experienced in my life.

I am grateful for the amazing potential the future holds.

I am grateful for this moment right here, right now.

I am grateful for the people in my life.

I am grateful for everyone who loves me.

I am grateful for everyone who challenges me.

I am grateful for the wonders of mother nature.

I am grateful for plants and animals.

I am grateful for the wind and the weather.

I am grateful for all my skills and talents.

I am grateful for endless opportunities.

I am grateful for the abundance I create.

I am grateful for the prosperity I attract.

I am grateful for the riches that flow into my life.

I am grateful for the presence of love in my life.

I am grateful for the full range of emotions I feel.

I am grateful for the things that excite me.

I am grateful for the many things that bring me joy.

I am grateful for this day teeming with potential.

I am grateful for another opportunity to serve and live life to the fullest.

I am grateful for being a beneficial presence on the planet.

I am grateful for all that I have.

Great job. I hope you fully embraced and embodied these affirmative statements. You truly are blessed.

And I hope your experience with these affirmations puts you in a great state to launch into your day. You've primed the pump. You've set the stage. Now go out there, enjoy yourself, and make amazing things happen.

Affirmations 2

POSITIVE MORNING AFFIRMATIONS

Start your day on the right foot.

First thing in the morning, right after you get out of bed, is the perfect time to set the tone for your entire day. This is when you can take control and lay a foundation that will influence exactly how your day unfolds.

In a moment, I will list some affirmations. In the space that follows, you can repeat them back to yourself, either out loud or in your mind. Or you can just sit in that space between and visualize and feel the feelings of that particular affirmation.

So if you're ready, let's begin.

I choose to feel good today.

I choose to express my joy today.

I choose to laugh today.

Today, I choose to be happy.

Today, I find goodness in unexpected places.

Today, I experience joy when I least expect it.

This is a really good day.

Today is full of potential.

I am so grateful for another opportunity to experience life.

Today is already a really good day.

Today is teeming with possibility.

What wonderful things await me on this glorious day.

I start this day with an open heart.

I begin this day with an open mind.

My vibration is high as I embark on this wonderful day.

Yes, this is a really good day.

I am so thankful for all the good in my life.

Today, I recognize the many blessings in my life.

Today, a sense of gratitude propels me.

This is a fabulous day.

Today, I feel awake, aware, and alive.

Today, I vibrate with confidence.

Today, I am the embodiment of success.

Today, I fully express my joy.

I begin this day with positive energy.

I launch into this day with optimism.

Today, I attract abundance.

Today, I attract prosperity.

This is a miraculous day.

This is a one-of-a-kind day.

Today, I celebrate life.

Today, I celebrate another opportunity to live, love, and serve.

This is a really good day.

Today, I am overflowing with energy.

I am overflowing with a sense of expectation.

This is my day to shine.

This is my day to take inspired action.

This is my day to make an impact.

Today is a wonderful day.

Today, I am fully present.

Oh, yes. This is an amazing day.

Now take this high vibration with you, and let it influence your attitude and your actions throughout the day.

Affirmations 3

WELCOME JOY INTO YOUR LIFE

You already know that affirmations can be very powerful.

But there are many ways to state affirmations. And all of these approaches to affirmations can work. They can be very effective, and I encourage you to try all of them.

However, with these affirmations, I want to try something different, and that is to take an angle of inviting the different qualities and the things that you want into your life.

It's not forcing them. It's not pulling them toward you. It's just being open and receptive. You're inviting them in. You're welcoming them into your life.

With these statements, we'll focus on joy, fun, positivity, pleasure, playfulness, laughter, and more.

So, if that sounds good to you, then take a deep breath in … followed by a long, slow, deep breath out.

One more time in … and out.

I will state each of these affirmations in three different ways.

In the space that follows, just repeat it back to yourself, either out loud or in your mind.

Let's start with joy.

I invite joy into my life.

I welcome joy into my life.

I am open and ready to receive joy into my life.

Let's not forget fun.

I invite fun into my life.

I welcome fun into my life.

I am open and ready to receive fun into my life.

And let's include another aspect of having an upbeat attitude with these affirmations.

I invite positivity and optimism into my life.

I welcome positivity and optimism into my life.

I am open and ready to receive positivity and optimism into my life.

Let's turn to pleasure.

I invite pleasure into my life.

I welcome pleasure into my life.

I am open and ready to experience pleasure in my life.

Let's address playfulness.

I invite playfulness into my life.

I welcome playfulness into my life.

I am open and ready to receive playfulness into my life.

This is an important one. Laughter.

I invite laughter into my life.

I welcome laughter into my life.

I am open and ready to experience laughter in my life.

Here's another good one: enchantment.

I invite enchantment into my life.

I welcome enchantment into my life.

I am open and ready to experience enchantment in my life.

Let's talk about creativity.

I invite creativity into my life.

I welcome creativity into my life.

I am open and ready to receive creativity into my life.

And how about energy and excitement? We could all use more of that.

I invite energy and excitement into my life.

I welcome energy and excitement into my life.

I am open and ready to receive energy and excitement into my life.

So what did you think of this approach to affirmations?

Being open, being receptive, inviting these qualities and these things and these people into your life. Welcoming them in.

It's a slightly different approach, but I think when you combine it with the other ways of doing affirmations, it can be pretty powerful.

So see how it works for you.

Recite these on a daily basis, on a regular basis for a while, or combine them with others.

As long as it's working for you, continue to do it daily.

I hope this was helpful. Wishing you an awesome day.

MORNING "I AM" AFFIRMATIONS FOR CONFIDENCE

Recite these affirmations every morning for 21 days in a row. Doing so will ingrain these powerful statements and help you feel and act more assured, assertive, and confident.

In the recorded version of this segment, I recite each affirmation, leaving you room to repeat it back to yourself, either out loud or in your mind.

The more emotion and enthusiasm you put into these affirmations, the more you'll get out of them.

Let's begin.

I am confident.

I am growing and changing for the better.

I am competent, smart, and capable.

I am worthy of all the good in my life.

I am confident in my abilities.

I am strong and powerful.

I am calm and comfortable in social situations.

I love the person I am becoming.

I acknowledge my self-worth.

My self-confidence is strong.

I boldly pursue what I want in life.

I believe in myself.

I calmly stand up for myself and my beliefs.

I confidently meet every challenge.

I speak my mind with respect for myself and others.

I express my thoughts and opinions with confidence.

I have steadfast confidence in myself.

Confidence is my nature.

Confidence is my birthright.

Confidence empowers me to take action.

Confidence allows me to live life to the fullest.

Being confident improves my life.

Feeling confident is simply who I am.

I enjoy being comfortable around others.

I move forward even when facing fear.

I am bold.

I am courageous.

I am positive and optimistic.

I am self-assured.

I am self-reliant.

I am upbeat and enthusiastic.

I am assertive.

I am calm and collected.

I am confident and composed.

I am poised.

I am cool.

I am comfortable in my own skin.

I am confidence personified!

I am secure.

I am brave.

I am valiant.

I am courageous.

I am safe and secure.

I am undaunted.

I believe in myself.

I bring value to the world.

I am worthy.

I am enough.

I am confident.

Again, to get the most out of these affirmations, I recommend you listen to them every morning for 21 days in a row.

After that, you can return to these affirmations whenever you need a boost of confidence and inspiration.

Thanks for reading. Have an awesome day.

POSITIVE AFFIRMATIONS FOR HEALTH AND HEALING

In this segment I list each affirmation. As you read each one, repeat it back to yourself, either out loud or in your mind.

Let's begin.

I am healthy.

I am perfect, whole, and complete.

I choose to be healthy.

I choose to be vibrant.

I choose to be whole.

Every cell in my body vibrates with life-giving energy.

My mind is sharp.

My body is in perfect working order.

I am healthy in mind, body, and spirit.

I am grateful for the healing that's happening right now.

I call forth perfect health.

I command healing energy to flow through me.

I let go of what doesn't serve me.

I give myself permission to heal.

I am healing inside and out.

I am patient with myself every day.

My body heals in its own time.

My body heals in divine order.

I am radiant, beautiful, and strong.

I believe in my ability to heal.

I deserve to be healthy.

I deserve to be happy.

I deserve to heal.

I deserve to live a full, vibrant life.

My body is a temple of health and healing.

My body is a magnet for wholeness.

Now is the time to be healthy.

Now is the time to be healed.

Now is the time to be whole.

My body is in perfect alignment.

My body knows how to heal itself.

My body knows what to do.

My body knows what it needs.

The cells of my body tingle with positivity.

I command my body to be healthy.

I command my body to be whole.

I command my body to find equilibrium.

I command my body to maintain and restore itself.

I listen to my body.

My body tells me what it needs.

I honor the wisdom of my body.

I trust my body to heal.

I love my body.

My body heals itself easily.

My body heals itself naturally.

My body is an intelligent energy system.

My body is a health-making machine.

My body is in harmony with itself.

My body is fueled by infinite intelligence.

My body is powered by infinite wisdom.

My body knows how to support itself.

My body knows how to sustain itself.

My body is attuned to the wisdom of the universe.

My body is in sync with nature.

My body is in harmony with the universe.

I am perfect, whole, and complete.

Great job. I wish you abundant, vibrant health. You deserve it. Have an awesome day.

AFFIRMATIONS TO ATTRACT LOVE AND RELATIONSHIPS

Say these affirmations every morning for 21 days in a row. Doing so will ingrain these powerful statements and help you attract genuine love and healthy relationships into your life.

The more emotion and enthusiasm you put into declaring these affirmations, the more you'll get out of them.

Let's begin.

I attract loving and caring people into my life.

I attract healthy, loving relationships.

I deserve to receive love in abundance.

I deserve a loving and caring partner.

I am thankful for the love that currently surrounds me.

I am thankful for the way I love and accept myself.

I happily give and receive love every day.

I happily invite love into my life.

I open my heart to love and know I deserve it.

I open my mind to amazing relationship possibilities.

Wherever I go, I find love.

Wherever I go, I am love.

I attract people who treat me with respect.

I attract people who are honest and kind.

I am worthy of being deeply loved.

I am worthy of being cherished and adored.

I deserve to be showered with affection.

I deserve a kind and caring lover.

I am grateful for my willingness to fall in love.

I am grateful for being open to love in its many forms.

I joyfully give myself permission to love.

I joyfully allow myself to give and receive love.

I open my heart to love.

I open my mind to make way for an amazing relationship.

I welcome a loving partner into my life.

I welcome a nurturing relationship into my life.

I am grateful for how loving I am.

I am grateful for how loved I am.

I enjoy comfortable, authentic relationships.

I deserve to feel safe and secure in a relationship.

I deserve to feel loved and honored.

I am worthy of a fulfilling relationship.

I am worthy of love.

Great job. And you know what, you truly are worthy of love.

As I mentioned before, to get the most out of these affirmations, go over this list every morning for 21 days in a row. You may be surprised by the results you get when you do it regularly.

After that, you can return to them whenever you need a reminder that you are worthy of the right relationship for you. One that's filled with joy, satisfaction, mutual respect, and deep personal fulfillment.

Affirmations 7

MORNING "I AM" AFFIRMATIONS FOR SUCCESS AND ABUNDANCE

In this segment I list each affirmation. You can repeat it back to yourself, either out loud or in your mind. The more emotion and enthusiasm you put into declaring these affirmations, the more you'll get out of them.

Let's begin.

I am prosperous.

I am abundant.

I am a prosperity magnet.

I bring immense value to the world.

I am rewarded for the value I create.

I recognize lucrative opportunities.

I act on my inspired ideas.

Prosperity is my nature.

Abundance is my birthright.

Wealth empowers me to make a difference.

Being prosperous allows me to make a positive impact on the world.

Being wealthy improves my life and the lives of others.

Abundance is simply who I am.

I have a wealth mindset.

I am grateful for the wealth I create.

Success and money come to me easily.

Money comes to me in expected and unexpected ways.

I am open and receptive to wealth of all kinds.

I embrace new streams of income.

I have an abundance mindset.

Wealth constantly flows into my life.

I welcome prosperity.

I am flourishing.

I am thriving.

I am success personified.

I am worthy of all the good in my life.

Great job. To get the most out of these affirmations, say them every morning for 21 days in a row. After that, you can return to them whenever you need a reminder that you are successful and abundant.

Have an awesome day.

FINAL THOUGHTS

Congratulations! You now have a more complete understanding of the power of affirmations. You know the impact that positive self-talk can have on your life. You now have the knowledge and are equipped with the tools.

The only thing that remains is to transform that understanding into direct experience. In other words, your next step is to put these principles you've learned into practice.

Starting today, carve out time every day, preferably in the morning soon after you get out of bed, for turbocharging your mind with affirmations. Say them, think them, write them, read them, and post them in places where you will see them throughout the day.

Go over them while you sit, walk, drive, or work out. Focus on the same set of affirmations or mix them up for variety. How and where you do them is up to you. The only aspect I encourage you to be strict with is the daily routine. Make affirmations a natural part of your day — every day!

Over time you will experience a shift in your mindset and attitude, which will soon lead to a surprising array of tangible results in your life. I've seen this pattern play out in my own life and in the lives of the many people around the world who visit my YouTube channel at www.YouTube.com/BobBaker.

So dive in and direct your thoughts toward the life you want to live. A richer, more fulfilling life awaits you.

ABOUT THE AUTHOR

Bob Baker is on a mission to inspire and empower people around the world. As an author, he spent decades helping musicians, artists, authors, and creative entrepreneurs use their talents and know-how to make a living and make a difference in the world.

In 2016, Bob started posting affirmation and meditation videos on YouTube. The channel grew and now serves hundreds of thousands of subscribers and attracts more than a million views per month.

He is the author of the highly acclaimed *Guerrilla Music Marketing Handbook* and many other books, including *The Empowered Artist*, *The Passion*

Principles, *The DIY Career Manifesto*, *Unleash the Artist Within*, and *Branding Yourself Online*. He also developed the "Music Marketing 101" course at Berkleemusic, the online continuing education division of Berklee College of Music.

Bob is an active musician, workshop leader, visual artist, actor, and former music magazine editor who teaches creative people how to get exposure, connect with fans, and increase their incomes through their artistic passions.

He also teaches and performs improv comedy and cowrote *The Improv Comedy Musician* with Laura Hall, the longtime pianist and musical director of *Whose Line Is It Anyway?*

Bob is also an active podcaster and blogger. You can contact Bob and learn more about his affirmation work at www.BobBakerInspiration.com.

Made in the USA
Columbia, SC
25 April 2021